Depression
and Back

We welcome you to visit www.ironzeal.com where you may:

1. Find support groups and other resources;

2. Purchase a DVD of Susan Polis Schutz's documentary, *The Misunderstood Epidemic: Depression,* as seen on PBS;

3. Send or post your comments.

Depression
and Back

A Poetic Journey
Through Depression and Recovery

SUSAN POLIS SCHUTZ

Blue Mountain Press™
Boulder, Colorado

This book is dedicated, with much gratitude, to Stephen, my loving, perfect husband, and Dr. L., my wise, understanding psychologist. I would not have gotten healthy without their caring and unwavering support.

Copyright © 2010 by Stephen Schutz and Susan Polis Schutz.

All rights reserved. No part of this publication may be reproduced, stored in a retrieval system or transmitted in any form or by any means, electronic, mechanical, photocopying, recording or otherwise, without the written permission of the publisher.

Library of Congress Catalog Card Number: 2009040689
ISBN: 978-1-59842-475-1

Blue Mountain Press is registered in U.S. Patent and Trademark Office.
Certain trademarks are used under license.

Printed in China.
First Printing: 2010

♻ This book is printed on recycled paper.

This book is printed on paper that has been specially produced to be acid free (neutral pH) and contains no groundwood or unbleached pulp. It conforms with the requirements of the American National Standards Institute, Inc., so as to ensure that this book will last and be enjoyed by future generations.

Library of Congress Cataloging-in-Publication Data

Schutz, Susan Polis.
  Depression and back : a poetic journey through depression and recovery / Susan Polis Schutz.
     p. cm.
  ISBN: 978-1-59842-475-1 (hard cover : alk. paper)   1. Depression, Mental—Poetry. I. Title.

PS3569.C556D47 2010
811'.6—dc22

                                                              2009040689
                                                                      CIP

Blue Mountain Arts, Inc.
P.O. Box 4549, Boulder, Colorado 80306

Contents

"I used to be
a blanket
without seams —
a silk cocoon
of happy dreams
Now I'm
a quilt —
no square the same —
a patchwork
of pleasure and pain"

Introduction

I've always had an incredibly positive and uplifting attitude, successfully forging ahead through all aspects of life... until three years ago. Then, much to my bewilderment, I crashed into a severe depression and "mental breakdown." Unable even to get out of bed, I was completely shocked. I didn't understand what depression was or how this could take over one's mind until it happened to me.

I kept a journal of poems during this entire time (except for when I was in bed and wasn't even able to pick up a pencil). Some of the poems I wrote about this darkest time were written later — after I started to feel a little better.

People who cared about me told me that I had to have outside help from a psychologist in order to get better. They also told me that perhaps I'd need medication.

Though I later gained a realization of some of what caused my breakdown, including a genetic disposition for depression, each person who suffers from depression has his or her own unique causes. There are as many specific reasons for depression as there are forms of depression.

Every single person, no matter what your income, job status, or personal life is like, can have this debilitating despair. The one unifying — and positive — component is that no matter how hopeless it feels, most people can eventually recover.

Like everything else in life, those people who work the hardest will reach their goals the quickest. So to hasten the process of recovering from depression and anxiety, people must try to learn as much about these afflictions as possible. They must also learn as much as possible about themselves, which often leads to adjusting bad attitudes, behaviors, and thought patterns. This examination of one's mind is best done by regularly seeing a professional psychologist or social worker. If medication is needed it must be taken diligently.

I now know that depression is an illness of the mind. If we have a physical illness we go to a doctor, listen to his or her advice, rest, take medicine if prescribed, and eventually often get better. Depression needs the same, if not more, respect, attention, and care as when the physical body is ill.

In my life, being depressed was by far the absolute worst I've ever felt. I was emotionally and physically exhausted and wanted to stay in bed all day with the blanket pulled over my head. I had moments of panic, confusion, and anxiety. My mind played games with me. I felt hopeless, frightened, and miserable, and I often felt nothing at all. I was mad at myself for being this way. I never thought I'd get better, despite my psychologist and everyone else assuring me that I would.

After what seemed like forever, but was actually only three years, I finally reached a point where I was usually not depressed. When I say "usually," it's because I do have good and bad days now. It is somewhat of a struggle not to fall into depression, but most of my days are good and that's what counts.

Today I am not the same person who had a breakdown three years ago. I have become a new and better person — more compassionate, open, self-understanding, and thankful.

According to the American College of Physicians, depression strikes one in four women and one in eight men sometime during their lifetimes. Clinical depression affects more than twenty-one million people in America annually. I hope this book proves that not only are they not alone but that most people can recover from this lonely affliction.

Susan Polis Schutz

DEPRESSION

When I first became depressed, I stayed in bed for three months with hopelessness, despair, fear, anxiety, panic, complete lethargy, exhaustion, and unhappiness. I didn't care about anything nor did I feel anything but torture, suffering, and utter pain. My mind was completely out of control.

Sometimes I was able to write how I felt, and other times I could barely pick up a pencil.

Sinking
scared
all alone
My brain is being taken over
Almost in another world
Need to sleep
Devoid of any
pleasure
purpose or
reason

Does anyone know
these completely
devastating feelings of
emptiness
fright
lethargy
hopelessness
all paralyzed
into a body of despair?

*Spiraling, twisting downward
into an abyss of darkness —
a state of nonexistence
devoid of feelings*

*A barricade surrounds my bed
forcing me to be alone —
too scared to break the wall
too out of control to even want to
too tired to open the door*

*Spiraling, twisting downward
into an overwhelming misery
and nothingness*

So tired
strained brain
doesn't feel sad or hollow
just sort of numb
needs a rest

So tired
submerged brain
flooded with liquids
needs to be dried out

So tired
delicate brain
overpowered
needs to relax

So tired
sturdy brain used to have so much energy
could run as far and fast as necessary
but now just walking is wearying
needs to be strengthened

My voice is a whisper —
not enough energy
I can't see people —
don't want to talk
I can't read —
not able to concentrate
I can't work —
way too lethargic
I can't play —
way too miserable
I can't get out of bed —
just want to sleep
to escape this uncontrollable suffering

Body in bed
frozen under layers of blankets
exhausted
all alone
shaking with overwhelming numbness
Something's gotten hold of me
Can't move

Head in pillow
buried in feathers of fear
aching with misery
Can't think
Can't feel
My mind doesn't belong to me
Maybe I'm dead

Can't
won't
unable to
pick up a pencil
and write about
how I feel

Out of control
Sick feeling in stomach
Shaky brain
This isn't me
but who is it?
Maybe it's chemical
Maybe it's genetic
Maybe it's exhaustion
But why is it so
out of control?

From the brain
to the stomach
sinking into nothingness
I love life
so why am I so
lifeless?

Shut Up, Doris Day!

Every time I used to hear
Doris Day singing "By the Light of the Silvery Moon"
I'd sort of dance around with joy
Today it was playing
and I heard myself say
"shut up, Doris Day!"

This poem is not in any way meant to discredit Doris Day.
It is about how she represented pure happiness.

Depression is
one of the worst things
a person can have
because it takes over
your mind and body
You can't see
You can't taste
You can't hear
You can't feel
If only that section of your brain
could be cut out
then you could get back
to normal
You could see
You could taste
You could hear
You could feel
and instead of being
brain-dead
you would be
brain-alive

I am so tired
Don't feel like doing anything
The sun is shining
The air is beautiful
and I barely care

I don't even know
why I am so miserable
but I am

Will this ever end?
when will I wake up
and feel like I used to?
I hate this
I hate this

*I always thought depression
could be willed away
I thought it was something
you brought on yourself
Now I can't believe
I ever doubted
that depression was real
It is horrifyingly real
I am sad that I had to
experience it myself
to realize this
and I apologize to all the
depressed people I've known
whom I didn't understand*

*What is this
that takes over my mind
with utter fright and
desolation
like an epilepsy of my mind
torturing all my thoughts?
where does it come from
this miserable invasion
that possesses my entire
being?*

Hollow
Empty
Sinking
Cracking
Shivering
Numbly lying in bed

I'm just living (barely)
in a fog
of tiredness and
apathy

I feel nothing
but dismay
I am emotionally
and physically
exhausted
The only thought I have
is that I wish it were
six months from now
when I might be feeling better

Hands tingle
Feet tingle
Lips tingle
Unbelievable!
Not only does my mind
play havoc with my thoughts
but it plays havoc with my body

There aren't adequate words
to describe how
non-feeling
I'm feeling

Waiting
Just waiting
to wake up from this abysmal abyss

Listening to a sweet voice
accompanied by a harp
I sit in hot, steamy water
high above the ground
right under the sky
overlooking the ocean

The clouds envelop me
and I float into their misty, gray whirl
I cry but know not why

A ray of light shines through
I sit up straight and see the reflection
as one wave lights up
but the rest are still dark
Again I cry and know not why

The sun appears briefly
peeking through the fog
and then disappears
There is a sheen at the rim
of some clouds
lifting up the sky
causing the waves
to shimmer with vibrancy
I cry but know not why

All of a sudden
the gray turns to pink
the sun is on fire
and the waves burn with brightness
And I cry
And I sigh
And it becomes silent and dark

I'm so mad at myself
for being like this
why can't I make myself
all better
and enjoy life?

What's it like to
NOT write
or to be depressed?
It's like
A robin
without a song
A hummingbird
without its flutter
A gardenia
without its smell
A rose
without its thorns
The sky
without its clouds
A rainbow
without its hues
A pen
without ink
A pencil
without paper
My thoughts
without words
My soul
without passion

PILLS AND THERAPY

I wanted so desperately to get better. I was advised to see a psychologist in order to figure out what was going on in my mind and body.

I knew how important it would be to find the right person, so I thought about the characteristics I'd want my therapist to have. I then asked someone I highly respected for the name of a psychologist with those characteristics. Subsequently I saw that psychologist three times a week for one year and then twice a week after that. I wrote about the progress and setbacks I endured while trying to understand what depression is, what had happened to me, and what I had to do to get some control over the situation.

I also knew that I would most likely have medications prescribed for me by a psychiatrist. Being a holistic-minded person who knew even less about psychiatric drugs than I did about therapy, I was petrified of "mind-altering" medications. Previously, I rarely even took aspirin and was even more opposed to taking prescription drugs. I was so miserable, however, that I decided I had to quickly get over these prejudices, so I started taking the medications that my psychiatrist prescribed. I was willing to do anything that would help me, and I worked hard to overcome this misery.

So petrified to take medicine
What will it do to my brain?
What will it do to my body?
Read the fine print
with all the possible side effects
Sounds awful
You'd have to be crazy to take this medication
Well — that's probably a close diagnosis
So I'll close my eyes
and swallow the blue pill
In the hands of fate

There sits Dr. L
She has all the qualities
of a perfect psychologist
she knows and understands humanity
has a deep knowledge of psychology and
a natural instinct for what is right and wrong
she is very
intelligent
caring
kind
professional
organized and giving

she deals with sadness
thunder and lightning
one story after another
and another and another
barely flinching
always helping —
the calm among all storms
we who learn from her are so fortunate
to have her as our
teacher
interpreter
comforter
confidante and cheerleader

Once I graduate with honors
from the Old Brown Cottage —
my psychologist's office —
I will thank her forever
for holding my hand

I sit with my therapist
as if I am nude
but wearing white gloves
She touches my heart
yet I cannot touch hers
She knows
everything about me
I know
nothing about her
But I do know
that she is
loving
compassionate
knowledgeable
sensitive and
patient
I take off
my white gloves
and touch her heart
just enough to understand
the essence of my therapist
and perhaps that is enough
because I completely trust her
and our relationship

The blue monster
pokes its hideous head
into my body
shakes every pore to the core
causing my brain to feel numb
my head to spiral downward
my limbs to tingle with fear
The blue monster
causes pain in every cell
and when he's finished
he finally leaves my withered body
for new conquests
It's now up to me to
try to repair the damage
If so I will make it a life quest
to slay the monster
so that no one ever has to suffer
from his attack again

I am so foggy
I sleepwalk
through the day
Can't follow any conversation
Can't even comprehend
the question
no less answer it
Can barely stay awake
A gray cloud
obliterates all
thoughts and emotions
Is this my medicine taking over my brain?
Or is it my depression?
I hope it is my medicine because that is fixable

Right now
how do I feel?
I feel like the world is on my chest
Heavy and burdened
I have
a lack of energy
to think about it
and a
lack of compassion
to understand it
So I just continue to not feel much

I see the tears
in your eyes
But please don't feel bad for me
Don't pity me
Don't tell me
to pick myself up
Please do
support me
Do understand depression
And do
love me unconditionally

My darling daughter is visiting us
My daughter whom I love so much
I don't want her to see me like this
I want her to see me the way I used to be —
happy
spontaneous
full of energy
vitality
and creativity
But it's so hard to pretend
So hard to have a real smile
And she is very perceptive
I don't want to burden her
or have her worry
I'll just see what happens

IRRATIONAL — Pills and Therapy

Propped up with pills and therapy
Why can't I prop up myself
like I used to
walking with my head held high
bushwhacking through any hardships
ending each day content and happy?

Propped up with pills and therapy
I feel like a bit of a fool —
weak for falling down and not getting over this
vulnerable
overwhelmed easily
teary
panicky
confused and scared
dependent on others rather than myself

A bolt of lightning
caused me to fall to the ground
leaving me in pain and shock
A truck hit me
and sent me flying
into unknown territories

The pills take one hand
Therapy takes the other
My perfect, steadfast lover holds my arms
and I stand again quite wobbly

But the electrical current
will always be inside me
and I can't send it back
no matter what I do

RATIONAL — Pills and Therapy

Propped up with pills and therapy
and whatever else I can do
in order to walk with my head held high
slowly and thoughtfully through hardships
ending each day content and happy

Propped up with pills and therapy
I'm weak but getting stronger
vulnerable
overwhelmed sometimes
teary once in a while
panicky
confused but learning a new understanding
scared
trying to be more independent
while being more open and empathetic with others

A bolt of lightning
caused me to fall to the ground
leaving me in pain and shock
A truck hit me
and sent me flying
into unknown territories

The pills take one hand
Therapy takes the other
My perfect, steadfast lover takes my arms
as I lean on a silver cane, a little more steady
knowing that I'll be able to walk by myself someday soon

The electrical current
will always be inside me
and I can't send it back
no matter what I do
but it will diminish in time

Tingly
whimpering
simpering
Pampering
Vulnerable
Dependent on a pill
to jar my brain to be stimulated
to relax my brain to be sedated
Dependent on the whim of my brain
Dependent on scheduled appointments
Dependent on therapy
Sad — can't cry
Happy — can't laugh
What is
wrong
with
me?

Yeah, yeah, yeah
I know that ultimately
I'll be a better person —
more sensitive
more empathetic
more caring
more introspective
more understanding
more thoughtful
Ultimately
I'll be happier
But for now
ultimately
feels like it
will never come
as I whimper in the present

My bed
Soft silk blanket
feathers my body
I am able to rest in comfort
Supple, fluffy mattress
We are able to bounce
with extreme pleasure
But
blanket pulled over my head
darkness
mattress quiet
King-size bed
a hideaway from life
when mentally ill

I'm not like them
At times
they have such severe symptoms —
they can't function
At times
I don't recognize them —
their faces are so contorted
At times
they are so forlorn —
there is no hope

Whom am I kidding?
At times
I am them

The bright red sun
is fully enclosed in the puffy layer of clouds
and I'm in the sky
miraculously watching it from above
My fate is in the pilot's hands
whose fate is in God's hands
I have no control over this flight
and that's how I must
live life
realizing that I have no control
over many things

Shocking, rocking
Struck by a bolt of lightning
Here I am
(always had a protective vest on)
shattered into
a mass of ashes
that need to be glued together
piece by piece and
reassembled

Broken people
Broken lives
Cracks in the earth —
buried beneath the fallen bricks
Rivers of water —
drowned in the streets
Shooting drugs —
numbing the reality of life
Murders in the towns
and wars in the world —
suffocating any heart left in us
Broken people
Broken lives
Trying to survive —
trying to stay alive
And here I am
just trying to think

So confused
Always thought I had the answers
Now my brain is tired
but awake enough to know
that I don't have the
answers
and that is scary
So confused

So tired
of fighting
of being downhearted
of trying to feel better
of having little joy
of not knowing what to do
of not being able to smile
of the stinking of my brain —
the sinking of my soul

Floating through nature
despite the magnificence of the mountains
despite the beauty of the ocean
Floating through each day
despite all I do
despite all I feel
The willow tree grabs my limbs
trying to raise them
to breathe life into them
so that I don't continue to float

Anxiety

Right now
the hands of the clock
are my master
I look at the clock directly
I look at the clock
from the corner
of my eye
I look at the clock
hoping I can escape the slow-moving hours
Why?

Right now
I don't know what to do
There is very little that
I want to do
I look at the clock
and the minutes
go by so slowly
Will it ever be bedtime?
I look at the TV
but have no idea what's on the screen
I think about not knowing what to do
and get more anxious
I wonder what's wrong with me

Where Am I?

*It's been exactly one year
since I started therapy
I am learning where I came from
but I'm not sure where I am now!*

*I've been taught to think beneath the surface —
to figure out
what I can't understand
My therapist would say
"Try to describe who you are
in order to find out where you are"*

*"No" my therapist would say
"those are just labels —
try again"*

Who am I?

*"No" my therapist would say
"still just labels —
dig deeper"*

Who am I?

*"That's a good start"
my therapist would say
"You are learning
and you'll continue to learn
Soon you will know
and understand
exactly where you are"*

The Game

Watching a movie
I wander into myself
with confusion
fright and panic
My mind is playing
a bad game with me
as I wonder if I am going to have
a recurrence of my bedridden depression
of one year ago
Rather than give in to this
I'll use what I learned in therapy
to figure out
what is making me feel this way
I'll try as hard as I can
to examine my feelings
And I hope to
win the game

Panic and Anxiety

The wise psychologist tells me
that when I have panicky feelings
my mind is "overwhelmed"

When this happens
she tells me I need to figure out what specific thoughts
are causing me to be overwhelmed
I need to understand these thoughts
face and confront them
and then decide how to address them

I find it hard to believe that this will alleviate
my uncontrollable pangs of stomach panic
but I'll try anything

Being new to this process
every time I feel panicky
I run thoughts through my mind
to see which ones provoke my anxiety
and I discover several that
immediately cause panging in my stomach

Proud of myself
I now try to understand these thoughts
but that is more difficult
So I move on to try to face and confront them
I visualize these thoughts over and over again
and tears come to my eyes
I think I've hit a nerve
Now I must decide how to address these thoughts
but I am unable to do this alone
I still need advice

But to my astonishment
my pangs of stomach panic are almost gone

Tchaikovsky

Sitting here with family
whom I love
All reading but me
I am pretending to read —
staring at the same page
as my stomach and brain
quiver with uncontrollable panic
I've been taught that this will stop
when I figure out and then confront
the thoughts beneath the panic

Turn the page —
I listen to Tchaikovsky's poignant, sad notes
thinking as deeply as I can
Scary feelings emerge
that I can't identify

Turn another page —
worried that I'm going to descend into fiction!
But that's not all —
worried about what else?

Turn another page —
MUST figure this out
Turn another page —
and another
and another
Still don't know
Getting more panicky

Turn another page —
It's hopeless...

Pass some thoughts through my head
to see which one provokes my stomach

Turn another page —
think I found it
Panic moves to my chest
I'm taught that now I MUST
confront these thoughts

Close the book —
can't pretend to read anymore
Make a fire
Gaze at the flames
Feel the heat
Try to hear the crackling
Think I'm deaf
Some tears behind my eyes
I feel like if I really let loose
my tears would put out the fire
but I can't do that
My brain ought to be happy
and ease up on my body
but it hasn't

Not good at this
All I've done is bring my thoughts
from way down to way up
and maybe I don't even know which way is up

Try one more time —
Shivering in my thoughts
I try to wrap myself
in them
around them
through them
Tchaikovsky sounds emotional but beautiful

What's wrong with me?
I'm still not right!
So I try to figure it out
I'm a little scared
I'm a little panicky
I'm a little gloomy
But what's underneath these words
I just don't know
and I'm so disappointed to be feeling this way
All of a sudden
I have that miserable, uncontrollable
sinking feeling in the bottom of my stomach
I want to go to sleep to escape it
I am tired today
and I know that tomorrow
I will probably feel better
The sinking feeling is now gone
and I don't have to go to sleep
BUT
what's wrong with me?
I am not right!

The fact that I could wake up
feeling so much better than the night before
is very encouraging
Now I know that
when I'm feeling terrible
it will subside

I know many people
who have been depressed
and they do come out of it

But I don't think I'm making progress
toward feeling better
I'm pretty miserable
It's taken over my brain

Fog

Sometimes I'm so
out of touch with
my feelings
that the only way I know if I'm happy or sad
is if I listen
to the same
beautiful, riveting song
I've listened to a thousand times before
If I have tears, I know I'm sad
If I sing, I know I'm happy
If I dance, I'm exhilarated
At least this cuts through the fog
to the light

I stare at my notebooks
I have nothing to write
I listen to my mind
I have nothing to say
I gaze into space
I have nothing to see
What is wrong with me?

A Revelation

A person can choose to die
or she can choose to live
I choose to live
So —
I can't live like I'm dead
I MUST
be alive every second
learn to give up fears and worries
accept that I can't control everything
and that worry is useless and harmful
never let myself stagnate or be apathetic and lethargic
never wake up and not look forward to the day
AND I MUST
appreciate and not take for granted all life's beauty
swim in passion
dance in excitement
cry tears of happiness
cry tears of sadness

Today —
I was afraid to show you
my revelation poem
because I feared that
it might jinx my revelation
or maybe this revelation won't last
or maybe it might go away
or maybe it's not the answer I've been looking for
or maybe I just can't do it
So to show that I could conquer my fear
I shared it with you and then others
And even if this revelation disappears tomorrow
the beauty and truth I had this moment
will never go away

The next day —
Yes it was a nice revelation
but not the whole story
because today
I have so much anxiety
and I know that
this is not the way to live
I wonder
if I will ever get rid of
this scary, helpless feeling

Beautiful aroma
of the lilacs of my childhood
brings me back to the hedges
intermingled with jasmine
surrounding our old wooden house
Such lovely fragrances and colors
as we'd climb the oak trees
It's hard to remember that kind of life

What's it like to see smiling people
and not envy them?
what's it like to touch something
and really feel it?
what's it like to really want to do something —
anything?
what's it like to not think of myself
and just enjoy whatever is happening?
what's it like to wake up
and look forward to whatever the day brings?
I forgot!

START OF RECOVERY

As I started the process of beginning to recover from my depression, I wrote poems about how I felt while undergoing behavioral and other types of therapy. I read books about depression and faulty thinking patterns that explained many different ways to view the world. I constantly thought about what was going on inside my mind and continued to discuss my feelings with my wise psychologist while slowly getting stronger. My psychiatrist had to keep changing my medications because some had side effects, but I wanted to get better and was willing to do anything.

Every day I'd have doubts about the medications I was taking and the process I was going through. My mind would often revert back to depression and anxiety, but I plowed ahead, trying so hard to return to a stable, healthy mental state.

Sometimes
I feel like a baby
shocked with a crippling stomachache
who can't control the sensation
and who can't explain it
except with tears

I feel like a baby
whose skin is raw
whose body is vulnerable
who doesn't understand anything
but love
who needs constant protection and guidance

I feel like a baby
who gets up the courage
to take its first step
but then falls down and crawls

I feel like a baby
who will cry and scream
who will sing and dance
who will learn and experiment
who eventually
will walk without help and grow up

Sometimes I wake up feeling great
But today — like some other days
I woke up feeling something I can't identify
It's not in the pit of my stomach
It's not in the form of a shiver
It is sort of a dullness
a lethargy
a gloominess
Can I gaze at the ocean now
to elevate my mood?

Everybody has their problems
Everybody has their joys
I'm as everybody as everybody
Anybody will suffer
Anybody can break down
I'm as anybody as anybody
Somebody will always rise above adversity
Somebody will always be strong and positive
I'm not as somebody as I used to be...
and I want to be again

You get up
You get knocked down
You get up again
You get knocked down again
You get up again and again
You get knocked down again and again
But you still get up
because you want to live
for the many enjoyable moments

Now I have to plan
what I'm going to be doing
each day
I never used to plan my days
I'd just wake up and start doing things
Perhaps I'll know that
I'm all better when I can have
a more spontaneous life again

It's a War

It's a battlefield out there
It's a battlefield in here
fighting with every cell
gore
misery
emptiness
panic
chaos
ugliness
confusion
darkness
death

Then
a song is heard out there
a song is heard in here
music of the mind
glory
lilting
peacefulness
soaring spirit
clarity
lightness
beauty
love
life

I am so tired of all this
Will it ever end?
I am much better than before —
I don't want to stay in bed
I have plenty of energy
I see people
My voice is strong
So I've come a long way
but there is an underlying
nagging, annoying
negativity, anxiety and lethargy
I'm consumed with myself
and nothing else
and that keeps me from
really enjoying life
Will time make me feel better?

Broken down
stripped of
elusive polyester fibers
of jagged, concealed
chemical origin
Sewing up
thread by thread
Hopefully mending into
veritable cashmere fibers
of stronger, softer
organic origin

It's so beautiful here
At the peak of the mountain
the spruce trees are silhouetted
against the dark sky
I sit in the rope hammock
gazing down at the
twinkling lights
Several deer dance
to the songs of the crickets
How can anyone
feel anything
but peace and serenity
in this magnificent environment?
Yet here I am
feeling the beauty of nature
kind of teary
and not feeling peace and serenity
What is wrong with me?

Who? Why?

A little immobilized
A little strange
A little slow
Not right
Who am I?
Why am I?
I'm so weary of all this

Raining in the Mountains Song

Raining in the mountains
Aspens' glistening drops
Fireplace crackling
so warmly
Experiencing magnificence
Singing and dancing
music — no inhibitions

Rain hidden inside me
touched something mournful
Let myself drift
internally
dramatically
Better than being static
but ever-so-confusing

And I wonder
and I ponder
what all this beauty means

Raining in the mountains
touched something mournful
Rising sunshine
warmly drifting
feeling nature
singing and dancing
so dramatically

High in the sky
looking down at the city
feeling like I am a part of the mountains —
weak and changing spontaneously like the aspen leaves
swaying to the rhythm of the air
remembering feeling like the strong, solid rocks
that fortify the mountain

High in the sky
listening to Beethoven's "Ghost Trio"
Florescent clouds approaching —
white cotton candy dancing so gracefully
I see a ghost in the cloud
I shut my eyes and a tear flows down my cheek
I feel the beauty of nature
I feel pain
The ghost in the cloud disappears
as it separates into little ribbons
of abstract fragments

High in the sky
listening to the haunting violin in Korngold's "Lied"
I shut my eyes
My lips quiver
A few more tears flow and I taste a salty drop
The wind blows on my face waking me from my past
A few tears again
I am weak, raw and vulnerable
This is so hard
I dry my eyes
as the blue dome above me gets darker
I will continue this long journey
I will climb until I reach the top
where the stately evergreens proudly stand

Why am I so downtrodden blue
when the clear dome is the same paradisiacal hue
and the birds seem to be talking to me?
"Listen carefully
Rise up
and fly away freely
Carry nothing
and drink the nectar of life
Flutter with the wind
and perch on the quietness of the leaves
Listen carefully
to the flute of tranquility"
I hear the notes
but the melody is discordant

Even though I have problems
I love life
So much
that I'm always terrified
of death
So much
that I'm always consumed
with death
I must
start living again
Living as a lover with life

Pushing myself to go to dinner with my old friends
Pushing because everyone tells me
that this is one way of curing depressive lethargy
Will I smile
and talk easily
or will I sit there in silence?
I will try to enjoy the evening
even though I'd rather be in bed
And so the evening dinner passed
and I passed the evening
in a pleasant state
but with the thought that I was pretending to be normal
and with the thought that no one could understand
my anxiety and depression
Why do I continue to feel this way?

No structure
and I just don't know what to do
other than to get into my comfortable bed
pull up my soft silk blanket
and rest, rest, rest
until my next appointment occurs
I can function
I can engage
But I'm consumed with
what to do
when I have nothing to do

Overwhelmed

I did this and that
I called him and her
I scheduled the schedulers
I planned the plan
I served the servers
I found the experts
I managed the managers
I situated the situation
to be the best it could
I controlled the controllers
to the extent I could
and let go of what I couldn't
I suffered with the sufferers
watched the watchers
emoted with the emoters
cried with the criers
empathized with the empathizers
pained with the pained
And now
I am mentally tired —
my brain overwhelmed —
but this isn't the time
to worry about myself

Reality?

Just as soon as my mind feels good
I start to think it is just wishful thinking —
a game I play
I feel strange and confused
I worry that I'm going to return
to uncontrollable sadness
or that I'm "crazy"
I have pangs of shaking
in my stomach
Maybe I need more time
Maybe I need more proof
Maybe I need to be told
over and over again
that my feeling good
is a reality —
a glow that will remain

I feel well
except I worry
that I might fall
into another
deep depression
and that being well
is only temporary
Sometimes I just want to rest
but I worry
that resting may mean
I'm depressed
so I don't rest

My brain is tired
My body is tired
Every part of me needs a rest
But I hate to rest
Will this feeling
ever lift?
Will I wake up tomorrow
feeling better?
Unbelievable
Today I feel great
compared to yesterday, that is
What does that mean?
No naps?
I noticed the sun shining
I was interested in some things
My mind was clearer
I "pushed" things to happen
I am far from "great"
but so much better than yesterday

I looked at myself
How ugly!
My mouth was in a downward frown
so I made my lips
perfectly straight
Then I moved my lips
into a slightly upward smile
I looked at myself
How nice!
I felt better

Ran away
into a hole
in the middle of Nowhere
No visitors
No hurt
No sadness
No soul piercing
No disturbance
Oblivious to all problems —
No storms
No clouds
I hide
but what do I seek?
In Nowhere
every day is
sameness
passionless
feelingless
sensationless
involvementless
The clock ticks
with nothingness
The alarm screams
jolting me awake
As I go outside
I feel some rain
I hear some thunder
I see some lightning
My body trembles with fervor
I crawl out of the hole
in Nowhere
and frantically fill it with rocks
I want to go back to Somewhere
the land of
everythingness

Just as soon as I think
I am getting stronger
something sets me off
and I feel overwhelmed
I must rest my brain
I must rest the tears hidden behind my eyes
This is
ridiculous
sad
weak
tiring
disappointing
I wonder when and if
I will ever be
permanently strong
At least I now know that
when my brain regains its energy
I'll be all right again —
until the next time

Am I really
coming out of this?
Or is this a
temporary peace?
Oh, if only
it is permanent
I'll make good use of my time
I'll be compassionate
I'll be productive
I'll be loving
I'll be helpful
I'll be thankful

One day, okay
another day, terrible
Mood swings
that sometimes are intolerable
like today
Frantic nerves
despondent mind
Same person
Same medication
Same body
Yet so different
One day, okay
another day, terrible
but with the knowledge that if I can get through the day
tomorrow will be better

Last night I celebrated
as I declared myself not depressed anymore
It was the most wonderful feeling
I was happy, grateful, looking forward to things
and I relished in being normal
Today I woke up
I decided to try harder
to incorporate all I've learned
so my depression won't come back
I took my medicine
I concentrated on the present
I faced problematic situations
I tried not to think about myself
I even exercised
But today is difficult
and I know that
I celebrated too early

It's so hard
to fill up my hours
I often
don't know what to do
or I just don't want to do anything
so I do nothing
I can only think
but it's a circuitous
thought pattern
concentrating on me
It's so hard
living this way

Premonition Dream

Yellow roses
in every corner
on every table
A circle of sunshine
in a special room
decorated for me
"Why?" I ask
"We are celebrating your getting all better"
I smile
feeling really good
"It's about time" I say

Took a walk outside
blisters on every toe hurt
can barely stand
but I'm still smiling
I must really be cured
if I am smiling with
this amount of pain

And this vivid dream
will become a reality
someday soon

Fireworks

Swimming serenely under the electrified stars
the moon illuminates the ripples of periwinkle waves
transcending dreams
It is so beautifully divine

"What kind of fool am I"
to grieve about human complexities
to worry about superficial perceptions
to be frightened of my own essay
and to dwell on heartsickness?
Perhaps I am a benign fool!
No — that's not the whole story
I broke down
stripped of all I knew
flesh ripped from my mind
veins tangled and lost
pierced throughout
But now the wound is starting to heal

My brain —
slightly worn
slightly torn
very jagged
very frayed
Sewing it up
patching it up
thread by thread
Some break
some hold together
And my brain
tries to mend
though it won't be as strong as it used to be

Between birth and death
we live our stories
and sometimes I wonder
if it's worth turning the page
Other times I can't wait to
begin a new chapter
There are so many interesting
characters to meet
emotions to feel
places to understand
We need to live
every day of our lives
with vigor and zeal
before it's too late
so our own stories
will not be
that there are NO stories

I woke up
gazing at the
sun
fighting to
dissipate the
mist
over the ocean
and I wondered
if the
sun
would win today's battle
against the
mist
in my head

Volcano

Pressure builds
Earth can't hold it in anymore
Liquids scalding
Solids violently shattering
Fires exploding through the crust
destroying the old landscape
burning the mountain to the ground
which eventually will be built up again
and the few seeds that survived
will have more room to grow
than ever before

*R*ace, race, race —
such an unreasonable pace
Waves come to shore
and I wonder when the noisy storms will begin
Flowers start to bloom
and I begin to plan next year's
more complicated garden
I finish singing one song
and immediately sing another
When will I learn
NOT to jump into the future?
Soon it will be over
and all I'll have done
is to have run, run, run
When will I learn
to enjoy the moment
and the quiet peaceful tone
of the current melody?

The Race

*B*rain running in circles
The race has started again
Stomach continually pangs with anxiety
Legs tired and painful
Brain confused
Direction unknown
I'll run as fast as I can
or perhaps I'll just walk
If I pass the finish line
maybe there won't be any more races
and I'll be able to settle down

The weather
frames the day
and our mood
frames the mind
The sun or rain
can sink or raise our thoughts
as laughter or crying
can affect the atmosphere
It's a matter of how we react
how we think
what we envision
But it's the weather inside us
that rules our reality

I remember so many
first days of summer —
the warm breezes
ready to take me
wherever I might float
that day —
so free

Now the
first days of summer
are no longer free
I am burdened with
thoughts that ache
and I can no longer
float with the breezes
Yet I still love the first days of summer

The sun
strongly beats down on me
causing my body to dissipate some of its
sickly physical influenza
The mountain trees
sway ever so gently
The orange and black butterflies
dance gracefully on the flowers
The dandelion cotton
swirls around the dry air
The peacefulness
causes my mind to dissipate some of its
sickly mental angst
Can nature's quiet sanatorium
calm all ills?

I'm hibernating
amidst some warm rocks and feathers
Feels so nice as I doze off to rest
Found a soft corner
sometimes veering to the other corner
sometimes gazing out the hole
to see the wonderful view
but quickly going back into my own torpid state
getting fatter and
more comfortable each day
Soon it will be summer
and I hope to emerge
all charged up
ready to take on life
from all corners

I'm just faking life
Conversations fly over my understanding
Smiles are merely physical
Talk is minimal
Everything is just there —
outside my feelings
And I'm just
floating along
Hopefully tomorrow
I'll be able to swim

RECOVERY

Though it seemed like forever, after three years, I finally reached a point where I was usually not depressed anymore. The combination of therapy, medication, time, and understanding all contributed to my recovery. And in my own particular case, the support I received from my family, therapist, and friends was invaluable to my recovery.

I now look forward to most days and appreciate life's beauty. I'm passionate about music, people, and nature the way I used to be. I'm dancing again.

I am alive
thank you
thank you
thank you
thank you
thank you
thank you
thank you
thank you
thank you
thank you
thank you
thank you
thank you
thank you
thank you
thank you
thank you
thank you
thank you
thank you
thank you
thank you
thank you
thank you
thank you
thank you
thank you
thank you
thank you
thank you
thank you

Babbling Idiot

I went to a bakery
famous for its apple pies —
rhubarb, strawberry, blueberry pies everywhere —
permeating the air
Though I thought they'd say "no"
I asked anyway
"Do you make apple pies without sugar?"
I was quite surprised and apparently animated
when the woman said "yes"
And I was embarrassed when the man in back
of me said laughingly
"You sure are excited about this"
I feel like Rip Van Winkle
waking up after his long sleep

I am so happy
to be able to
talk to people once again
It's been so long
When I listen to music
I hear more notes
When I drive my car
it is such a good ride
When I walk on the beach
the ocean is more majestic
When a salesperson is efficient and nice
I appreciate her attitude and competence so much
When I interact with my family
I realize — every minute
how lucky I am to have them
Though I am not completely myself yet
I am improving every day
and in some ways I am better than before
I'll never take anything for granted

Sitting under a wooden roof
No walls but windy air
Surrounded by the heaviest rain I've ever seen
The purple weeds
are bent to the ground
The noisy drops form
hundreds of jumping fountains on the sidewalk
The splashes of water
are so fierce
they bounce into the hut
My feet are wet but warm
Thunder travels through the sky
and the sun is out
despite the storm
And the sun is out
despite the storm

I can be strong
when things are going well
But the real test of strength
is how one reacts
during a difficult time
Will I collapse in
weakness and irrationality
as soon as something difficult happens
that I don't understand
can't control
or I think is sad?
Have I experienced enough
learned enough
felt enough
to be strong enough
to rationally accept
things that are not going well?

My living room
is THE "room with a view"
The sky, the trees...
It's home to my music
Memories arise of sitting on
the round leather couch
listening to Chopin
as I orbited into the clouds —
so contentedly dancing to the Rolling Stones
spontaneously and rhythmically —
so high-spirited

For a while
I didn't want to enter —
couldn't enter —
this sanctuary
It was too beautiful and peaceful
too full of grace
for my sad and scared mind
So full of despair
I couldn't relate to tranquility
I was out of touch with reality
but most of all I was too unhappy
to be in a happy place

Now at least I want to be in that room
but I am afraid of destroying it with my tears
so I challenged myself
to see if I could regain the serenity of
my living room
I blasted the music
to drown out my thoughts

Though I was shaky
and felt my face contorted
my living room
still has a view
And maybe next week
I'll dance

It's a gorgeous day
The demons can't take that away
The air is brisk
The ocean still
I only smell freshness
I only see beauty
Nature is majestic
The demons can't take that away

The window lights twinkle below
The haze around the moon shines
luminescently on the crashing waves
It is so serene
so quiet
so peaceful
Is this the same world
I was so apathetic toward?

I Can Feel Again

I've been broken
and beaten down —
all jumbled up
shaken and undressed
trying to get back into
my tuxedo of life
I weep in silence when I see beauty
I weep in silence when I see pathos
I am an emotion
within a tear

I used to be so curious
about everything
My eyes were
alive with wonder
Why do fireflies
light up?
How do rainbows
make such beautiful colors?
What hardness
is each rock I find?
How old
is the tree I'm looking at?
What is the uniqueness of every state?
Now I'm not curious about anything
My eyes
are closed
with dullness
Has this been brought about by depression?
Yet I am newly curious about
what is in one's heart
Has this been brought about by depression?

The mountains collide in a beehive shape
In the far background
the snow dots the summit
and the clear blue sky
surrounds all the majesticness
How can I —
such a tiny part of the world —
think I am so important
as to complain?

My emotions are raw
empathizing continuously

My mind is raw
seeking new understanding

My brain is raw
overflowing with words
to be written

My body is raw
exploding ardently

Elusive tears of sadness
tears of joy
tears of delirium

It took depression
to ultimately create passion

I Lament Myself

Whitman brilliantly said
"I celebrate myself"
Today not so brilliantly I said
"I lament myself"

I am the sick with tubes and lifesaving devices
I am the homeless living on the streets
I am the soldier whose buddy was killed
I am the woman with three jobs
I am the man with no job
I am the child being picked on
I am the kid with no parents
I am the baby crying for help
I am the victim in an earthquake
I am the person addicted to drugs
I am the "crazy" in a mental ward
I am the lawbreaker in prison
I am the mother on welfare
I am one huge tear
But tomorrow I hope to say
"I celebrate myself"

I Celebrate Myself

Walt whitman brilliantly said
"I celebrate myself"
Yesterday
I lamented myself
Today
I, too, "celebrate myself"
I am the wife who loves and appreciates her husband with
     every fiber of her soul
I am the passionate lover
I am the flutist in the orchestra
I am the dancer in the ballet
I am the farmer watering the growing vegetables
I am the politician fighting to help people
I am the actress nervous about her first performance
I am the kid in the sandbox
I am the athlete running around the track
I am the patient thankful for medical advances
I am the man putting out fires
I am the woman helping her neighbor
I am the protester expressing her outrage
I am the author writing her truth
I am the singer baring her emotions
I am the worker proud of her job
I am the pupil learning and growing
I am the baseball player who just hit a home run
I am the baby sucking my thumb
I am the toddler taking her first step
I am the sister to everyone
I am the mother of all children
I am the woman whose family is the most important part of her life
I am the good friend with very strong relationships
I am the opening petals of a rose
Yesterday
I lamented myself and life
but today
"I celebrate myself" and life

93

The Mild Storm

I survived the windy storm —
just getting a little wet
and slightly bruised
but standing up straight
knowing how to take shelter
and clean up the debris
I think that
I won't need to run away from the sunshine
or fear the next mild storm
My mind is starting to become
stronger and more energetic
I can hear the beautiful music

I think I feel
like my normal self again
but my normal self
has changed

I feel beauty mystically
but with a tinge of sadness —
because there is no pure beauty

I feel music so passionately
but with a tinge of tears —
because in the music I hear the minor key

I feel life deeply
but with a tinge of despair —
because much of life is unkind

I feel more connected to all people
but with a tinge of gnawing compassion —
because I understand anguish

I feel more connected to myself
but with a tinge of new vulnerability —
because my emotions are raw

My mind has been badly bruised and torn apart
Perhaps it needed to be hurt
so it could recover
to become more whole
to fully feel

I must be stronger than I think I am
I'm still tolerating my depression
I'm still trying to fight it
Every day is a struggle
Yet I continue this struggle
without giving up
although this moment I feel like giving up

Like a corked bottle of sparkling wine
water held back by a dam
a dog with a muzzle on its mouth
my writings are inside, somewhere
dying to get out
I taste the wine
I let the water pass through its barrier
I throw off the dog's muzzle
But I can't muster up
the creativity hidden in my brain

Don't understand why I'm so glum
Don't understand how everyone can smile
Don't understand why
I can't smile
Don't understand how
I can tolerate this
I thought I was "all cured!"

Thank you but
don't worry about me
I'm okay
at least a good part of the time
And when I'm not okay
there's nothing you can do anyway
except love me
understand me
support me
That's more than enough
and I thank you

I had a nice day
I — who rarely knows the difference —
had a nice day
I heard the waves of the ocean
I felt the notes of the song
I smelled the humidity in the air
I dug my feet into the sand as I walked
    on the beach
I read on my cool sheets under my
    comforting silk blanket
And though I still am unable to say
    I had a great day
I had a nice day
And that sure was nice

If most of the time
I am not
panicky
self-absorbed
obsessed
negative
worrying
weak
doom filled and
overwhelmed
the sun will have
eclipsed
the darkness
and I will realize that
everything I've gone through —
all that I've learned and changed —
will have been essential
to the person I've become

Sometimes
in the midst of
my depression
I wonder
how the day will pass
I don't want to
do anything
I just want to
lie in bed
But miraculously
time continues and
night finally comes
I go to sleep
Another day
has passed

I'm so glad that this day is over
I can hide under my
silk blanket
and go to sleep
I can get away from my
mental anguish
and relax my brain
I can have eight hours of peace
and hopefully wake up feeling better

There is blood on the streets
from all the burdens
Heads cracked open inside —
stooped beneath shoulders outside
Abandoned people in winter jackets
in the heat of summer, talking to themselves
Stenches permeate from dark alleys
Scraggly puppies follow scraggly owners
Drunks fall off curbs
Garbage in the streets
Garbage in the minds
Bald man with preppy jacket
turns the key to an apartment —
his story
Heavy woman in shabby dress
clothespins her husband's, son's, lover's, relatives' shorts —
her story
Hospitals, jails, shelters, streets — house stories
Mountains, hotels, schools, mansions are homes to other stories
And there is wine on our tongues
from all our passions
Heads buoyed in the clouds by life's beauty
Melodic crescendos bring morning and evening rhapsodies
throughout our bodies
that explode in fireworks — so out of control —
to an outside delirium
dancing to the rhythm of love
Smell of the retracting storm
Sounds of the birds talking to one another
Sights of the aspen trees waltzing in the wind
The words of the understanding and caring
The stories are mixed
The stories are hard
The stories are panic
To feel the short ecstatic moments —
they are all more than worth living for

The Conductor

I'm conducting the symphony
Free up the emotive sound of the flutes
Tone down the weeping violins
More notes from the laughing bassoon
Lighten up the rumbling drums
Increase the passionate sax
Bring in another lilting vibe
Add more powerful bass
Strengthen the fragile harps
Extend the range of the smooth piano
Dramatize the clarinet

I'm conducting the orchestra
Unshackle the beat
The sound is just the way I want it to be
and the music is beautiful

I've been shaken up —
Flying pieces
shattered
scattered
battered
Settled pieces
torn
worn
newborn
Repaired pieces
bent
befriended
amended

Some days
I see the sun
melt over the ocean
and it's just the
ending to another day —
nothing more

Other days
I stare at the bright red hue
at sunset's magnificence
and it's a mystical, overpowering emotion —
nothing less

A Pause

My words from three years ago —
I was a miserable
beyond body and mind
not in control of anything
dysfunctional
dreadful
mess

My words from yesterday —
I was a scared
recovering
searching
raw
functional
weak
child

My words from today —
I am a sensitive
vulnerable
confused
dependent
learning
student

My words for tomorrow —
I will be a growing
strong
happy and sad
grasper of my feelings and life
mostly peaceful
dependent and independent
woman
who knows who she is
and where she's going

One Never Knows Song

The drums dance
the triangles ring
in our new call —
our new act
A time to be bold
A time to be different
A time to be ourselves

No more coasting along
It's time to live our dreams
As we've sadly seen
if we don't do this right now
one never knows

The drums snare
the triangles ring
in our new call —
our new act
A time to be helpful
A time to be caring
A time to be loving
A time to embrace life
A time to be

No more coasting along
It's time to live our dreams
As we've sadly seen
if we don't do this right now
one never knows...

It's time to live our dreams

Dancing on a Rock

On a crest of a rock
above the ocean
a couple
with their arms around each other
dance dramatically
to the rhythm
of the waves
A little girl stares
at them perplexed
and says to her mother
"They are so silly!"

I am that kind of silly —
that kind of spontaneous

I savor all winds of life
and am not much worried
about clouds too high to reach
at least not today
and hopefully
not tomorrow

The soft, spotless snow paints
a glistening white polish
on the tall oak trees
As it begins to melt
I notice the leafless branches
so barren
so lifeless
And I wonder... why?
But soon
the buds of growth start to bloom
new green life appears
and it's clear!
Only in the
most naked state
where the weight of the splendid leaves
is shed
can the trees
be vitally reinvigorated for the new
joyful season

The sun has chosen one cloud
to cast its fading light upon
This golden brilliance wakens the darkness
How can one be oblivious to life?

I went to the bottom
of the bottom —
a pure mental hell
Please don't let me go
there again
I've been so battered
I need time to cry
I need time to laugh
I need time to get
reacquainted with life

*S*ometimes others' woes
are too much for me to bear
Sometimes my own woes
are too much for me to bear
But I am a fighter
who will tear apart
the clouds
to see the sun

Coming Home Song

I'm a little lost child
so tired of the storm
Up, up and down
round and round
How long must I roam?
When will I follow the right path to my home?

I see
wounded people, wounded lives
hearts that suffer, souls that cry
wounded people, wounded lives
everybody just trying to survive

So here I am now
with tears in my eyes under the fiery sky
with reflections of the moon
but not feeling peace
and having my doubts
trying to figure it all out

I see
mending people, mending lives
hearts with passion, souls with joy
mending people, mending lives
They gaze at the ocean and swim above the waves

I've suffered enough
I want to see the sun
I want to hear the laughter
I want to feel the beauty
I will write my own music and get rid of the pain
I'll no longer roam
Finally, I'm on the right path home

I think
I finally feel normal again
but it's an altered normal —
a new normal
one that is arduous to espouse
I used to be
a blanket
without seams —
a silk cocoon
of happy dreams
Now I'm
a quilt —
no square the same —
a patchwork
of pleasure and pain

I can get out of bed in the morning
I don't have a
paralyzed mind
Each day is different
and many days are a struggle
But I've come back
I understand what depression is
I understand that I will always have good and bad days
I understand that this is the way things are
I am very appreciative of the progress I have made

Good Morning

Good morning
to me
a person that I am just getting to know
awakened to a new life of thunderstorms
as well as sunshine
who sees
with an understanding eye
full of tears for
sadness and difficulties
as well as for
joy and passion

ABOUT SUSAN POLIS SCHUTZ

Susan Polis Schutz is an accomplished writer, poet, documentary filmmaker, and advocate for women's issues, the elderly, and dispelling the stigma of mental illness. She is a graduate of Rider University where she majored in English and biology and was later awarded an honorary Doctor of Laws degree. Together with her husband and creative partner, Stephen Schutz, she co-founded Blue Mountain Arts, a popular publisher known for its distinctive greeting cards, gifts, and poetry books.

Susan is the author of many best-selling books of poetry illustrated by Stephen. Her first book, *Come Into the Mountains, Dear Friend,* was an instant success. It was followed by many more titles, including *To My Daughter with Love on the Important Things in Life,* which has sold over 1.6 million copies and led *Time* magazine to proclaim her "the reigning star" in high emotion. Its companion volume, *To My Son with Love,* has also enjoyed a wide audience. Susan's poems and Stephen's artwork have been published on over 425 million greeting cards worldwide.

Following the tragic events of September 11, 2001, the Schutzes created a small book of Susan's poetry and Stephen's artwork entitled *One World, One Heart.* It was distributed free to over seven million people throughout the world with the hope that Susan's words would encourage people everywhere to put aside their differences and come together in peace, understanding, and love.

Susan's latest undertaking is creating documentary films that make a difference in people's lives with her production company, IronZeal Films. Her films have been shown on PBS stations throughout the country and include *Anyone and Everyone,* which features a diverse group of parents and their gay children discussing their experiences, and *Following Dreams,* which tells the stories of people who have overcome all odds and misfortunes to pursue their life dreams. Her latest documentary, *The Misunderstood Epidemic: Depression,* seeks to bring greater attention to this debilitating illness and to help people and family members understand and empathize with individuals affected by depression.

For more information on
The Misunderstood Epidemic: Depression,
a documentary by Susan Polis Schutz
that is being aired on PBS,
please visit www.ironzeal.com.